I Love to F*cking Color! And Relax with My Swear Word Adult Coloring Book.
Copyright 2016 by Don Cummings

ISBN-13: 978-1530170296
ISBN-10: 153017029X

F*ck Off! I'm Coloring Series
First Edition Volume Two 2016

20 Unique Swear Word Designs!

All Illustrations Are Printed Twice! Double The Fun!

Every Design Is On A Separate Piece Of Paper! No Bleed Through!

Hours And Hours Of Relaxation! Excellent Stress Relief!

Use Your Own Coloring Tools! Crayons, Colored Pencils, Or Markers!

Start Coloring Right Away!

Fuck Yeah!!!